OHIO STATE BUCKEYES

BY CRAIG ELLENPORT

Published by The Child's World®
1980 Lookout Drive • Mankato, MN 56003-1705
800-599-READ • www.childsworld.com

Cover: AP Photo/Jay LaPrete.
Interior: Newscom: Icon SMI 8; Robert Seals/TSN 11; Mike Cardew/KRT 19; Robin Alam/Icon Sportswire. Shutterstock: aceshot1 4; Barry Salmons 12 top; Jamie Lamor Thompson 12 bottom, 15, 16; 1. Wikimedia: 7 (2).

ISBN 9781503850378 (Reinforced Library Binding)
ISBN 9781503850637 (Portable Document Format)
ISBN 9781503851399 (Online Multi-user eBook)
LCCN: 2021930301

Printed in the United States of America

Two Ohio State defenders celebrate a big play.

CONTENTS

WHY WE LOVE COLLEGE FOOTBALL

Just about everybody in the state of Ohio loves football! There are two pro football teams in Ohio. Fans cheer for the Cleveland Browns or the Cincinnati Bengals. Most people in Ohio agree on one favorite college football team. That's the Ohio State University Buckeyes!

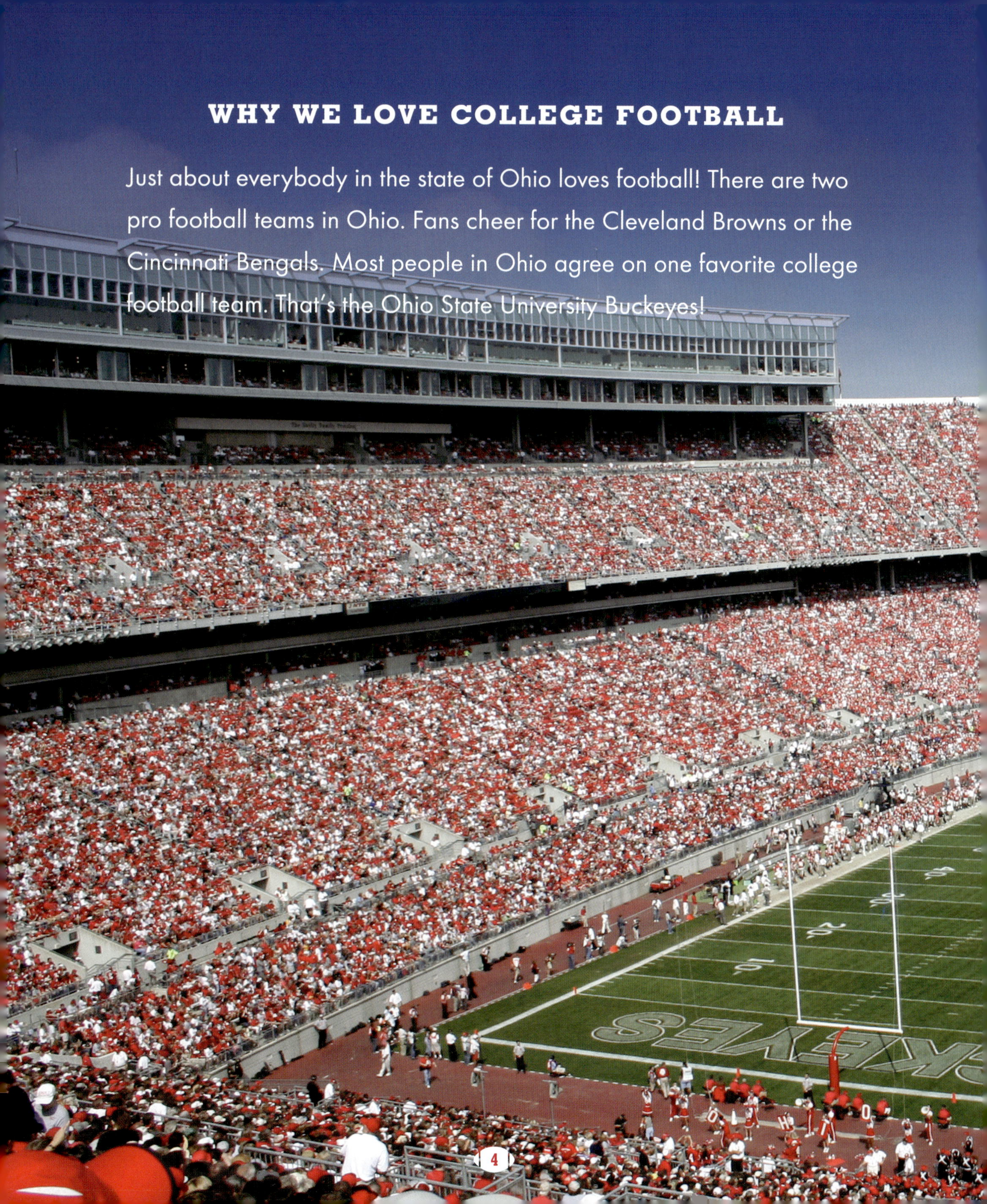

Ohio Stadium is one of the largest—and loudest—fields in the country

The Buckeyes are one of the best schools in college football history. Ohio State fans are very proud of their team. They call their school *THE* Ohio State University. Let's learn more about the Buckeyes.

CHAPTER ONE

Early Days

Ohio State football began in 1890. The first coach was Alexander Lilly. In 1912, Ohio State joined the Big Ten **Conference**. Ohio State's first star player was Chic Harley. He led Ohio State to Big Ten championships in 1916 and 1917.

In 1941, Paul Brown became the head coach. In 1942, the Buckeyes won the national championship! In 1946, Brown left OSU. He helped start a new pro football team. It was named for him—the Cleveland Browns!

WHY BUCKEYES?

The buckeye tree is the official tree of the state of Ohio. Ohio became the "Buckeye State" in the 1840s. In 1840, Ohio's William Henry Harrison was elected president. He called people from Ohio "Buckeyes." The nickname stuck!

***Above:* Look how much rounder the football was in this 1890 OSU team photo.**

***Right:* The 1897 team looked sharp, but didn't play well. They won one game and lost seven.**

CHAPTER TWO

2

Glory Years

The Buckeyes have won eight national championships. The first came in 1942.

In 1951, Woody Hayes was named head coach. Under Hayes, Ohio State won five national championships (1954, 1957, 1961, 1968, and 1970)! Hayes always worked his team hard during practice. His Buckeyes were tough to beat.

NO. 2 IN WINS

Through 2020, Ohio State had won 929 games. That's the second-most ever! The Buckeyes have won the Big Ten title 39 times, too.

Hayes left in 1978. Ohio State was still very good. They finally won another national championship in 2002. They won it again in 2014.

Left: Woody Hayes' Buckeyes won a total of 206 games. He also won five Coach of the Year awards.

CHAPTER THREE 3

Best Year Ever!

In 2002, Ohio State had a historic season. They won 14 games. They were the first college team to do that!

Ohio State started out 13-0. They played Miami for the national championship. Ohio State was not expected to win. Miami had won 34 games in a row. The Buckeyes battled! It was a very close game.

The game was tied 24–24. Then the fourth quarter ended! In **overtime**, Maurice Clarett scored a touchdown. Ohio State won, 31–24. The Buckeyes were 14–0 and national champions!

Right:* *The powerful running of Maurice Clarett (13) was key to OSU's win over Miami—for the national title!

BUCKEYES

Above: It's a great honor to be chosen to "dot the i" (circle) in the band's formation.

Left: Brutus Buckeye has been helping OSU fans cheer since 1965.

CHAPTER FOUR

4

Ohio State Traditions

Ohio State has one of the sport's greatest marching bands. During **halftime**, fans love to watch them. The band has a famous routine. Marching in a line, they spell out O-H-I-O in script lettering.

One band member gets to "dot the i" in Ohio. Sometimes Ohio State invites special guests. Astronaut John Glenn, entertainer Bob Hope, and golfer Jack Nicklaus have all "dotted the i."

Ohio State's mascot is Brutus Buckeye. A student wears Brutus' giant foam head and striped sweater.

THE BIG RIVAL

Ohio State versus Michigan is one of the college football's biggest **rivalries**. Fans call it "The Game." They have played each other since 1887. Michigan leads the series 58–51. There have been six ties, too.

CHAPTER FIVE

5

Helmet Stickers

What are all those little circles on Ohio State helmets? They are buckeyes.

In 1968, Woody Hayes gave players a new reward. He handed out stickers to players after they played well. The tradition was born. Today, players still work hard to earn those stickers. The best players can cover their helmets with stickers!

THE HORSESHOE

The Buckeyes play at Ohio Stadium. The stadium opened in 1922. Today, it seats more than 100,000 fans. Ohio Stadium is shaped like a giant letter "U." It is nicknamed "The Horseshoe."

The more stickers a player has, the more successful he has been!

WARNING
9
CKEYES

6

CHAPTER SIX

Top Ohio State QBs

Les Horvath was Ohio State's first great quarterback. In 1942, he led OSU to its first national title. In 1944, he won the **Heisman Trophy**.

TROY SMITH'S HEISMAN

In 2006, quarterback Troy Smith led the Buckeyes to a 12-1 record. He threw 30 touchdown passes. He won the Heisman Trophy!

J.T. Barrett holds many Ohio State passing records. He played from 2014 to 2017. Barrett passed for a school-record 9,434 yards.

In 2018, Dwayne Haskins had a fantastic season. He passed for 4,831 yards and 50 TDs. Both are OSU records for one season.

In 2019, Justin Fields threw 41 TD passes. In 2020, he led the Buckeyes to the national championship game. They lost, but it was a great season.

Left: Justin Fields has 63 TD passes in his first two seasons leading OSU.

7

CHAPTER SEVEN

Other Ohio State Heroes

There have been 86 Heisman Trophy winners. Only one player has won the award twice. That was Ohio State running back Archie Griffin. Griffin won the Heisman in 1974 and 1975.

Eddie George was another great Buckeyes running back. In 1995, he set a school record with 1,927 rushing yards. George won the Heisman Trophy, too.

Chris Spielman was one of the school's best **linebackers**. Spielman was a tackling machine! He won the Lombardi Trophy in 1987. That award goes to the best defensive player in the country.

OHIO STATE'S HEISMAN TROPHY WINNERS

Les Horvath, 1944
Vic Janowicz, 1950
Howard Cassady, 1955
Archie Griffin, 1974 and 1975
Eddie George, 1995
Troy Smith, 2006

In 1995, Eddie George led the Big Ten in rushing yards. He was tops in the nation in touchdowns scored, too.

HAMPTON
11
WILDCATS
8
VAPOR

CHAPTER 8 EIGHT

Recent Superstars

On defense and offense, Ohio State has seen some great players in recent years. In 2014, Joey Bosa had 13.5 **sacks**. He was named Big Ten Defensive Player of the Year. In 2017, Nick Bosa had 8.5 sacks. Brothers Joey and Nick were both first-round picks in the **NFL draft**.

In 2019, defensive end Chase Young had an incredible season. He set an Ohio State record with 16.5 sacks. He forced seven **fumbles**.

In 2020, running back Trey Sermon set an OSU record. In the Big Ten Championship Game against Northwestern, he rushed for 331 yards. That was a new team record for one game!

Who will be the next star to add to Ohio State's great history?

Left:* *Up and over! Trey Sermon hurdled over a defender during a long run in the 2020 Big Ten Championship Game.

GLOSSARY

conference (KON-fur-enss) a group of schools that play sports against each other

fumble (FUM-bul) when a football is dropped and can be recovered by any player

halftime (HAFF-tyme) the midpoint of a football game

Heisman Trophy (HYZ-man TROH-fee) award given each year to college football's best player

linebacker (LYNE-bak-er) position in the middle of the defense

NFL draft (N-F-L DRAFT) annual event in which NFL teams select college players to play for them

overtime (OH-vur-tyme) extra playing time if the score is tied at the end of a game

rivalries (RY-vul-reez) rivalries happen when certain teams face each other often, usually over a long period of time

sack (SAK) a play where the defense tackles the quarterback before he has a chance to pass

FIND OUT MORE

IN THE LIBRARY

Cooper, Robert. *College Football.* Minneapolis: Discover Roo, 2020.

Hunter, Tony. *Ohio State Buckeyes.* Minneapolis: Lerner, 2020.

Kelly, Danny. *The Scarlet Cleat.* Herndon, VA: Mascot Books, 2017.

Weber, Margaret. *Ohio State Buckeyes.* Toronto: Weigl, 2020.

ON THE WEB

Visit our website for links about the **Ohio State Buckeyes**:
childsworld.com/links

Note to Parents, Teachers, and Librarians: We routinely verify our Web links to make sure they are safe and active sites. So encourage your readers to check them out!

INDEX

ABOUT THE AUTHOR

Craig Ellenport is the author of many sports books for young readers. He went to Northwestern University, but his Wildcats didn't quite make it into this series!